IMAM
AL-MAHDI
(A)

14

HEAVENLY CHILDREN

The Valuable Gift

Kisa Kids Publications

Dedication

This book is dedicated to the beloved Imām of our time (AJ). May Allāh (swt) hasten his reappearance and help u
to become his true companions.

Acknowledgements

Prophet Muḥammad (s): The pen of a writer is mightier than the blood of a martyr.

True reward lies with Allāh, but we would like to sincerely thank the efforts of Shaykh Salim Yusufali, Brother Aliakba
Shaheidari, Sisters Sabika Mithani, Fatemah Mithani, Amna Hussain, Asieh Zarghami, Zahra Sabur, Sajeda Merchan
Kisae Nazar, Sarah Assaf, Nadia Dossani, Fathema Abidi, Fatemeh Eslami, Fatima Hussain, Fatemah Meghj
Sukaena Kalyan, and Zehra Abbas. We would especially like to thank Nainava Publications for their contributions
May Allāh bless them in this world and the next.

Preface

*Prophet Muḥammad (s): Nurture and raise your children in the best way. Raise them with the love of the Prophet
and the Ahlul Bayt (a).*

Literature is an influential form of media that often shapes the thoughts and views of an entire generation. Therefore
in order to establish an Islāmic foundation for the future generations, there is a dire need for compelling Islami
literature. Over the past several years, this need has become increasingly prevalent throughout Islāmic centers an
schools everywhere. Due to the growing dissonance between parents, children, society, and the teachings of Islār
and the Ahlul Bayt (a), this need has become even more pressing. Al-Kisa Foundation, along with its subsidiary, Kis
Kids Publications, was conceived in an effort to help bridge this gap with the guidance of ʿulamah and the help c
educators. We would like to make this a communal effort and platform. Therefore, we sincerely welcome constructiv
feedback and help in any capacity.

The goal of the *Heavenly Children* series is to foster the love of Ahlul Bayt (a) in children and to help them establis
the 14 Maʿṣūmīn as their role models. We hope that you and your children enjoy these books and use them as
means to achieve this goal, inshāʾAllāh.

We pray to Allāh to give us the strength and *tawfīq* to perform our duties and responsibilities.

With Duʾās,
Nabi R. Mir (Abidi)

Disclaimer: Religious texts have ***not*** been translated verbatim so as to meet the developmental and comprehensio
needs of children.

Kisa Kids Publications
4415 Fortran Court
San Jose, CA 95134
(260) KISA-KID [547-2543]

Ahmad, Mama, and Baba had spent the whole afternoon talking about their upcoming ziyarat trip to visit the fourteen Ma'soomeen.

"I know the last Ma'soomeen we will visit! It's our twelfth Imam (AJ)!" Ahmad said. "I know he's alive, so we can go visit him, right?"

"Well, Imam Muhammad al-Mahdi (AJ) is alive and is always guiding us, but we cannot go visit him because we don't know exactly where he is. He is in *ghaybah*."

"What's *ghaybah*?" Ahmad asked.

"*Ghaybah* means 'occultation,' which means becoming hidden. The *ghaybah* is divided into two time periods: *Al-Ghaybah as-Sughra* and *Al-Ghaybah al-Kubra*."

"What's the difference between the two?" Ahmad asked.

"*Al-Ghaybah as-Sughra*, the smaller occultation, took place from when the Imam (AJ) was five years old and lasted for 68 years. Although the exact location of the Imam was kept secret, he would answer people's questions through his four representatives." Mama explained. "*Al-Ghaybah al-Kubra*, or the greater occultation, began after the Imam's fourth representative died, and still continues to this day."

"Why is his location hidden, though?" Ahmad asked.

"Remember all those times that the caliphs poisoned the Imams, or the people stood against the Imams? Well, because the people aren't ready to follow the Imam (AJ) and support him in his work, Allah has kept him safe until the people are willing and ready to stand for the mission of Islam under the Imam's guidance," Baba said. Ahmad sat thinking about this for a minute.

Mama added, "Remember when the Imam (AJ) was born on the 15th of Sha'baan, his father kept him hidden?" Ahmad nodded. "His father, Imam al-Askari (a) only told a few close companions about the Imam (AJ). The caliphs knew that the twelfth Imam (AJ) would spread peace and justice, which means he would put an end to their corrupt rule. After leading the funeral prayers of his father, Imam al-Mahdi (AJ) went into *ghaybah*. He will come back once he has enough followers to help him spread peace and justice."

"Can I be one of his followers?" Ahmad asked eagerly.

"InshaAllah!" Baba said. "InshaAllah, we can all do good deeds, make good choices, and prepare ourselves to be his followers and companions!"

Ahmad became quiet again. "How are we going to visit him?"

Baba responded, "Although we do not have to go anywhere to visit him — really, we can talk to him wherever we are — we will visit Masjid al-Jamkaran in Iran, which is the masjid of our Imam (AJ)." Ahmad's face brightened, glad to hear this.

His father said, "Let me tell you a great story about another Ahmad, who was a companion of our beloved Imam (AJ)!"

As Ahmad finished his speech, the crowd's eyes filled with tears of wonder and awe. Ahmad was a strong believer, and his words were filled with his deep faith in Allah. Such sincere words had a powerful effect on the listeners.

People flocked around him now, handing him letters and gifts that they wanted him to deliver to Imam Hasan al-Askari (a). They had come from so many faraway places to the city of Qom, just so they could have their gifts delivered to their Imam (a)! Many did not even know Ahmad personally, but they trusted him with their precious parcels. Ahmad carefully packed all the letters and gifts into the side of his horse's saddle.

He mounted his horse, took hold of the reins, and bid farewell to all the believers.

As Ahmad's horse began trotting through the village, an old woman came running out, waving a small woven cloth. "Wait, wait, dear boy, wait!" she cried out.

Ahmad stopped in front of her and got down from his horse and the woman handed him the cloth. "Dear son, please take this gift to the Imam (a) on my behalf. I have weaved it with my own hands!" she said.

Ahmad took the woven cloth. He couldn't help but notice that it was very small and plain. The old woman read the disappointment in Ahmad's face. "Dear son," she said, "I know it's not much, but I have hope that my Imam (a) will accept it, and maybe, just maybe, he may pray on it even once."

Ahmad nodded, ashamed of his reaction, and placed the woven cloth with the rest of the gifts. Now, Ahmad was ready to begin his journey. The crowd watched as he departed, wishing that they were also young and strong enough to visit their Imam (a).

After travelling for many days, Ahmad finally made it to the city of Samarra. As he entered the city, he was overwhelmed by the hustle and bustle. The streets were filled with people coming and going in all directions.

This was very different than the small, quiet city of Qom. After asking around, Ahmad got directions to the Imam's house, and quickly found his way there.

As he reached the simple home, his heart began to race. He was finally about to meet the Imam (a)!

Ahmad descended from his horse, hoisted the bundle of gifts, and knocked on the door.

The Imam (a) opened the door with a warm smile on his face. "Salaamun Alaikum," he said.

Upon seeing the Imam (a), Ahmad's heart fluttered. He wiped the tears from his eyes and replied, "Wa Alaikum Salaam!"

He hugged the Imam (a) tightly and kissed his hands.

The Imam (a) led him into a room and sat behind a desk, where he had been writing a letter. Next to him sat a beautiful child, no more than three years old. The child was paying very close attention to what his father was doing.

Ahmad placed the Imam's gifts and letters on the floor. "O son of Rasulullah (s)," he said, "I have come all the way from the city of Qom! I have many questions to ask you, if you will allow me!"

The Imam (a) smiled, pointed towards the small child, and kindly said, "Dear Ahmad, please ask my son Mahdi your questions."

Ahmad was surprised, but he knew the Imam (a) did everything for a reason, so he sat next to the small child. His heart stopped as he realized that he was sitting before the final Imam (AJ)!

He bent over and kissed the young Imam (AJ) on his head. "O my Imam," he said, "may my father and mother be sacrificed for you!* I have been waiting so patiently to see you! I thank Allah for this great blessing!"

*In our ahadith and du'as, when someone wants to show the highest level of loyalty and love towards another person, they use this expression.

The young Imam (AJ) answered each of Ahmad's questions with wisdom and virtue. Satisfied, Ahmad turned towards Imam al-Askari (a). He motioned towards the bundle and said, "O Imam, the people of Qom have sent you these gifts and letters."

Imam al-Askari (a) said, "Dear Ahmad, please take out the gifts and letters, and place them next to my son." Ahmad did so.

The young Imam (AJ) looked through the gifts one by one. Suddenly, he asked, "O Ahmad, where is the gift that the old woman gave you?"

Ahmad blinked. Quickly he searched through the items, but he couldn't find it! Beads of sweat began forming on his forehead. How irresponsible of him! He felt very anxious to have lost a gift, and the one that he had looked down on, too!

He apologized to the Imam (AJ). "Perhaps her gift is still in the saddle of my horse. I will go look for it right now!" he said, jumping up to go check.

Ahmad rushed out the door and rummaged through his horse's saddle bags. He looked through all his luggage, tossing things, desperate to find the gift that the Imam (AJ) had requested. There was no sign of the woven gift! Upset with himself, he thought, *I can't believe I lost it!*

Empty handed, Ahmad walked back into the Imam's home with a bowed head. He felt ashamed at his error. But he looked up to an amazing sight! The young Imam al-Mahdi (AJ) was sitting on the woven cloth, reciting prayers!

"SubhaanAllah," Ahmad marveled. The old woman's sincere du'a had been answered by Allah! Ahmad felt humbled and honored to witness the answering of her du'a. Her gift may have seemed simple, but her *ikhlaas* — pure intention — made it the most valuable gift of all!

Biḥār ul-Anwār, Vol. 52, P. 80